MARY CARTER SMITH

African-American Storyteller

Babs Bell Hajdusiewicz

—Multicultural Junior Biographies—

ENSLOW PUBLISHERS, INC.

44 Fadem Road	P.O. Box 38
Box 699	Aldershot
Springfield, N.J. 07081	Hants GU12 6BP
U.S.A.	U.K.

Library of Congress Cataloging-in-Publication Data

Hajdusiewicz, Babs Bell, 1944-
     Mary Carter Smith, African-American storyteller / Babs Bell Hajdusiewicz.
        p. cm. — (Multicultural junior biographies)
     Summary: A biography of the Afro-American woman who gained fame as a
storyteller and became "America's Mother Griot" or official storyteller of African
stories.
     ISBN 0-89490-636-4
     1. Smith, Mary Carter—Biography—Juvenile literature. 2. Afro-American
women authors—20th century—Biography—Juvenile literature. 3. Storytellers—
United States—Biography—Juvenile literature. [1. Smith, Mary Carter.
2. Authors, American. 3. Storytellers. 4. Women—Biography. 5. Afro-
Americans—Biography.] I. Title. II. Series.
PS3569.M53776Z69 1995
818'.5409—dc20
[B]   95-8688
                                            CIP
                                            AC

Printed in the United States of America

10 9 8 7 6 5 4 3 2 1

Illustration Credits: Copyright ©, Afro-American Newspapers Archives and Research Center, Inc. 1991. Reprinted with Permission., p. 60; From Mary Carter Smith's personal collection, pp. 8, 13, 17, 27, 34, 37, 39, 48, 69, 75, 78; Photo by Gordon H. Stills, Baltimore, p. 76; Photography by Jeffery A. Salter, © 1994, p. 74.

Cover Photograph: Cover photograph of the storyteller Mary Carter Smith telling her folktale "Cindy Ellie" for the *American Storytelling Video Series*, Volume Five. Produced by Storytel Enterprises. Distributed by the H.W. Wilson Company. Copyright © 1986 by Storytel Enterprises.

CONTENTS

Acknowledgments

The author expresses gratitude to Gail Blasser Riley, attorney and author, for encouragement and selfless sharing of the many facets of her expertise; Marie Howard Adams, Miracle Banks, Richard Banks, Yvonne Banks, Dr. Rebecca Carroll, Kooki Davis, Sally Ghee, Wendell Green, Yvette Thomas Wellons Hector, Mary Sawyer Jones, Fellisco Keeling, Dr. E. Lee Lassiter, Paulette McAlily, Reverend P.M. Smith, Joan Simmons Stephenson, Clearman Sutton, Wilnetta Sutton, and Sam Wilson for sharing their past and present memories; to Chris MacGregor for photograph restorations; and to Sally Goodroe Bates and Brenda Weir, storytellers/librarians, Houston Public Library; Cary Beth Cryor, *Baltimore Afro-American* newspaper archivist; Catherine Foster, Public Relations Assistant, Baltimore Public Schools; Susan Frost, Coordinator of Youth Programs, Baltimore Symphony Orchestra; Becky Montalvo, Business Office, Youngstown City Schools, Youngstown, Ohio; Barbara Napfel, Assistant to President, Morgan State University; Diana Shagla, Mahoning Valley Historical Society, Youngstown, Ohio; Gail Stanfield, Assistant to President, Coppin State College; and Joan Wolfe, Editor, *Newsday*, Long Island, New York for research assistance.

DEDICATION

This book is dedicated with love to all readers;
some young, others young at heart;
to Grace and Evan, my mother and late father,
and Harry, my stepfather,
for giving me wings;
to Jerry, my husband, for believing in stories and in me;
to Nick, my son, for reaching out to help others;
to Alison, my daughter, for caring and sharing;
and
to Mary Carter Smith, for touching us all.

A HURTFUL THING

Out of every race in the human race, certain individuals stand out.[1]

—Seymour Kopf, journalist

It was snowing in Ohio on the day before Christmas vacation. Eight-year-old Mary* and her classmates were excited.[2] They had a plan! Someone would give the signal. All the children would slide out of their seats and line up at the teacher's desk. One-by-one, the children would give their gifts to the teacher.

Mary held her gift tightly as she waited for her turn. She had shopped long and hard to make

---

* Mary Carter Smith, born Mary Rogers Ward, also used the names Mary Rogers Coleman and Mary Coleman Carter during her lifetime.

her choice. She had carefully wrapped her gift in tissue paper and pretty ribbon.

Mary thought her turn would never come.[3] She watched the teacher's face as other children gave their presents. With each child, it was the same routine.

The teacher smiled and opened the present. Then she smiled again and said a special "thank you." Finally, it was Mary's turn. She took a deep breath and proudly handed her gift to the teacher.[4]

Mary watched the teacher's face. She waited for the teacher to smile.[5]

But there was no smile. Instead Mary watched as her teacher's frowning face turned red. The teacher held Mary's present by one corner "as if it was something filthy."[6] Her

Mary Rogers Ward is shown here at age three.

fingers barely touched the lovely white handkerchief with its pink edging. The teacher lifted the handkerchief from the wrapping and held it high above the trash can beside her desk. Mary watched in painful silence as the teacher dropped her present in the trash.[7] Then, the teacher quickly looked over Mary's head to the little white girl behind her, and smiled.[8]

Young Mary stumbled to her seat. She knew that she must never leave school until she was dismissed. So she sat in silence until the school day was over. Then she rushed out of the building and ran all the way home. Sobbing, she asked her grandmother, "Why did she do that to me?"[9]

"Mama," as Mary called her grandmother, sat down beside the warm oven in the kitchen. She pulled her granddaughter onto her lap. "Child, you are Colored," Mama explained, "and that makes a big difference to some people."[10] Mary had noticed that her own skin was darker than anyone else's in her classroom. But this was the first time Mary had realized that the color of a person's skin could cause others to say or do hurtful things.[11]

As always Mama Nowden was there to hug young Mary. But over the years, Mama Nowden gave her granddaughter more than just hugs. Mama Nowden comforted five-year-old Mary when the girl's mother was murdered. Mama Nowden taught Mary to care about other people—no matter how old the people were, or what color they were, or even how they acted. Mama Nowden always told stories and sang songs to young Mary. Mama Nowden encouraged Mary to read. She said, "Child, learn that book. Nobody can take that away from you."[12]

Mama Nowden had planted the seeds for the choices Mary would make throughout her life—"to build bridges between people," even when that meant coming face-to-face with the woman who had murdered her only child.[13]

FAMILY TIES

Though I was surrounded by those who loved me, my life was not without hurt and pain.[1]

—Mary Carter Smith

Mary Carter Smith was born on February 10, 1919. She was given the name Mary Rogers Ward. Her parents, Eartha Nowden and Rogers Ward, had been in love. But Eartha's mother, Mary Deas Nowden, would not allow them to marry. Mama Nowden felt that Rogers Ward could not be a good husband to her seventeen-year-old daughter.[2]

Mary's Mother Marrries

Eartha Nowden and her baby lived with Eartha's family. The Nowdens lived in a little house behind a church in Birmingham, Alabama. When Mary was four years old, her mother married Warren Coleman. Mary became known as Mary Rogers Coleman.

"I loved my sick daddy. He was good to me," Mary said about her stepfather.[3] She knew him for only a short time before he died of a lung disease called tuberculosis.

Mary's Mother Marries Again

Early in 1924 Mary's mother married again. This time Eartha married a man named Earl Knight. Some people said he was "mean."[4] Eartha planned to join her new husband in New York City. She wanted to take young Mary with her.[5] But Mama Nowden asked her daughter and son-in-law to leave Mary behind until they were more settled.

When Eartha left for New York, young Mary stayed in Birmingham with her grandmother and uncles—Anderson "Brother" Nowden and Jackson "Buddy" Nowden McQueen. Many years later

Mary found a letter her mother had written while in New York. "How is my baby?" Eartha had asked Mama Nowden in the letter. "She is the darling of my life."[6]

Jobs were hard to find in the South in the years following World War I. So Mary's uncles soon left Birmingham to go north. When her sons moved, Mama Nowden stayed behind with young Mary. Sixteen-year-old Brother found a job in the steel mills in Youngstown, Ohio. He then rented a house and invited his mother and his niece to join him. It was there, on October 27, 1924, that the Nowden family learned about Eartha's tragic death. Her new husband Earl Knight had shot her.

From left to right, Eartha Nowden, Mary Deas Nowden, and Anderson "Brother" Nowden are shown here.

Dealing with Grief

Mary was not tall enough to see into her mother's casket. So someone lifted her. She stared at Eartha Nowden Knight's still body. Mary remembered the pretty woman who had held her and sung to her in the little house back in Birmingham, Alabama.[7] During the funeral, everyone patted Mary on the head and said, "You poor little thing!"[8] They then gave her money. Mary liked getting money. She liked it so much that she wanted more.[9] So she set out to get just that.[10]

She marched out into the street near her home. There she told the first of many stories that she would tell during her life. She cried out the sad tale of how her mother had been murdered in New York City. People listened and felt sorry for Mary.[11] Then the strangers gave her money!

Mary's story had impressed her audience on the street. It did not, however, impress her grandmother.[12] When Mama Nowden learned what Mary had done, she spanked her. She warned her granddaughter never to do such a thing again.

Special Flowers

Mary and her grandmother often vistited Eartha's grave. Mary would always remember the pansies she laid on her mothers's grave. She called the pansies "flowers with faces."[13] Though her mother had died, Mary still had her aunts and uncles and Mama Nowden. She would later write:

> My family is the soil from which I grew. And in that soil, I grew to love stories—all kinds of stories. . . . I often stood at my grandmother's elbow . . . she opened the big family Bible and read to me in her soft voice.[14]

Years later, Mary Carter Smith would have Mama Nowden's family Bible restored. In 1985 she gave the Bible to the Enoch Pratt Library of Baltimore, Maryland.

In 1925 the Nowdens moved to another house in Youngstown, Ohio. Next door to the house was a lumber yard. Mary and her friends hauled scraps of wood to Mary's yard. Then they built a playhouse. Mama Nowden gave the children real food to take out to their house. The playhouse made a perfect stage for Mary. She tried out all kinds of stories on her friends. She told stories that she'd read and heard. Sometimes she even made up stories![15]

A Good Student

Mary was a good student at Shehy Elementary School. She remembers how one of her teachers there encouraged her to do her best: "Miss Gilbert told me I was smart and that I'd be 'Somebody' some day."[16]

Mary once wrote about a substitute teacher at the elementary school, "Miss Showalter told my class wonderful stories about George Washington Carver and Booker T. Washington. That was the first time I had heard of anyone my color doing anything worthwhile."[17]

Reading a Book Every Day

Mary began to spend hour after hour in the public library. Soon she was reading a book every day. She had heard Miss Showalter tell stories about African Americans. But Mary couldn't find any of those stories in the library. Stories about African Americans were missing![18]

Still, Mary was learning about her history at home. African Americans filled her grandmother's stories. She especially liked the stories about when Mama Nowden was a little girl.[19] Mary also read her uncle's books. One book, *Your History*, had stories and pictures about African Americans.

Mary read all the time at home. When Mama Nowden called, "Mary Rogers, time to go to bed!" Mary did just that.[20] She got right under the covers —with her book and a flashlight!

Mary Rogers Coleman, age eight, sits at her desk at school.

"That Good Reader"

Mary's classmates at Shehy noticed how much she read. They noticed how well she read. Soon they began to call Mary "That Good Reader."[21] Even so, Mary sometimes had to defend herself. She was the only African-American person in her class. One Columbus Day, a second-grade classmate taunted her about her heritage. "We Italians discovered America," bragged the Italian boy. "All you people did was pick cotton."[22]

Mary felt hurt and angry. She was confused about what to say or do.[23] So she struck out with her fists. "We had a big fight, and I won!"[24]

Special Summers

Summers during the 1920s were special for Mary. She went to visit her aunts, Eartha's sisters. They lived in small coal-mining towns in Pennsylvania and West Virginia.

Everyone in Mary's family called her aunts by their nicknames. Willie Nowden McAdory was called "Aunt Booby." Sally Lou Nowden Coleman was "Aunt Teady." Delia Nowden Simmons was known as "Aunt Cookie." Mary loved and admired her aunts.[25] Her aunts adored their niece as well.[26]

Summer days with her aunts meant Mary got to ride in Aunt Cookie's car. She loved to listen to the stories and songs Aunt Teady shared. She also loved going to parties with her aunts.[27] World War I had ended, and people in America were happy. They danced and sang with joy during those exciting years known as the "Roaring Twenties."

At the parties, Mary had her second taste of being paid to perform. She danced and danced and danced. She danced the Charleston, the Snake Hips, and other dances that were popular at that time. People gathered around her and threw money! "I was the Charleston Champ!" she exclaims.[28]

Moving to West Virginia

In 1927 Mary's uncles found better-paying jobs in New Jersey. Brother and Buddy worked as Pullman porters for a railroad company. They helped passengers with their luggage. When her sons left Youngstown, Mama Nowden and eight-year-old Mary went to live with Aunt Teady in Grant Town, West Virginia. But Mama Nowden missed her little house in Birmingham.[29] So in less than a year, Mary and her grandmother moved back to that house.

Life was peaceful for almost two years. But tragedy struck again in 1930. Mary was eleven years old when Mama Nowden became very ill. Mary's aunts rushed to Birmingham to pack up Mama's and Mary's things. This time Mary and her grandmother would go to live with Aunt Booby in Edwight, West Virginia.*

* The town of Edwight, West Virginia was situated near Whitesville, but it no longer appears on maps.

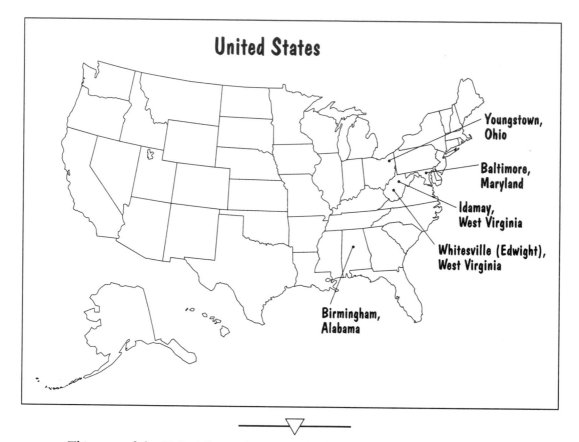

United States

Youngstown, Ohio

Baltimore, Maryland

Idamay, West Virginia

Whitesville (Edwight), West Virginia

Birmingham, Alabama

This map of the United States shows cities and towns where Mary Carter Smith and her family lived.

Mama Nowden and Mary left their little house in Birmingham. They would never return.

Part of American History

Mary lived in Edwight for nearly three years. The small coal-mining town was often called a "coal-field." During her years there, Mary was part of an important event in American history.

In 1931 nine young black men were accused of attacking white women in Scottsboro, Alabama. The McAdorys read all about the "Scottsboro Nine Case" in the newspaper. They read about how people were sending money to help pay lawyers' fees for the nine young men accused of the crimes. So Mary made and sold paper flowers. Then she sent some of the money that she earned to the "Scottsboro Nine."[30]

The "Scottsboro Nine Case" was also called *Powell* v. *Alabama*. The case went all the way to the U.S. Supreme Court. The highest court in the United States made an important law. The Court ruled that when poor people were accused of a crime, they had the right to have a lawyer and a fair trial.[31]

Music Fills the Air

Mary Carter Smith's childhood was filled with music. Mama Nowden had a piano that almost played itself! Mary would put paper rolls in the "player piano." Then she'd pump the piano's pedals. The keys would go up and down as if fingers were touching them! Music would fill the whole house.

People in coal-mining towns such as Edwight, West Virginia, still sang songs from the old days. "Lining-out" and "shape-note" singing had been popular in churches long ago during slavery times. Few churches had pianos then, and few people could read. But everyone sang!

Mary learned to sing the old songs too. In "lining-out" singing, someone read a line. Then Mary and the others repeated it. In "shape-note" singing every note, do-re-mi-fa-so-la-ti-do, was shown by a different shape. Mary would sing "la" when she saw a rectangle-shaped note. Then she would sing the song's word.[32] She also learned "verse-speaking." Her teachers at school taught the children to speak and sing together in verse-speaking choirs.

"Back to Africa"

Mary learned other skills while living in Edwight, West Virginia. She was a talker and a storyteller. But she was also a good listener. Aunt Booby's husband was a member of the Universal Negro Improvement Association (UNIA). The group had begun in the 1920s. Leader Marcus Garvey encouraged black people to leave the United States and return to Africa. Mary liked to listen when her uncle talked about the UNIA's "Back to Africa" activities.[33]

Mary's good listening skills also helped her to learn many new words. "I heard some colorful cussing on the 'coal-fields,'" she admits. "I remembered those words and even made up some 'do-lillys' myself!"[34]

Mary was a polite church-going child. But she found a way to use her new words. On Sunday afternoons after church, she and her girlfriends often hiked up the mountain outside of Edwight. Mary remembers the cussing contests she and her friends held on top of the mountain. "I always won, hands down!"[35]

Two years after the move to Aunt Booby's, Mary faced one of the greatest sorrows of her life. On May 18, 1932, Mama Nowden died of cancer.

Thirteen-year-old Mary lost the grandmother whom she had loved so dearly as her "Mama."[36]

Mary missed her grandmother. She missed Mama Nowden's hugs. She missed hearing Mama Nowden tell stories and sing songs. She also missed hearing Mama Nowden laugh.[37] But even in her sadness, Mary knew she still had her dear Aunt Booby.[38]

In 1933 Mary finished eighth grade in Edwight. For the most part, her life began to settle. But not for long. One night during her first year of high school, she and the McAdorys had to leave town.

"SOMEBODY"

She had such a keen sense of humor. She knew how to make people laugh even then.[1]

—Mary Sawyer Jones, high school classmate

Mary Carter Smith spent many of her student years in all-black schools. At that time, the "separate but equal" law applied in the United States. This meant that blacks and whites could be forced to go to separate schools—as long as children were given an equal education.[2]

Mary remembers the long days during her years at Leevale School in Edwight:

> I had to leave home extra early to be bussed down the highway. We passed a fine white school on our way to the little rickety black school. Each day

after school we had to wait for the white children
to ride the bus first. Then we were taken home.[3]

Years later Mary would also work in all-black
schools. In 1954 the U.S. Supreme Court ruled
that there was no such thing as "separate but
equal." The Court's famous decision *Brown* v.
Board of Education meant that students could no
longer be separated by skin color.[4] Still, Mary
would choose to work in inner-city schools,
where students were mostly African Americans.

Moving Upstate

Aunt Booby's husband Norman McAdory was a
coal miner. He was also an "organizer" for the
United Mine Workers union. He urged other
miners to join the union. The union members
worked together to make each mine a better
place to work.

Union organizers were not well-liked by mine
owners and managers. Because of this, Mary's
uncle was threatened by hired hoodlums known
as "goons."[5]

One night in 1934 the threats became serious.
Norman McAdory had to hurry his family out of
town. This time fifteen-year-old Mary and her

Mary Carter Smith spent most of her youth in all-black schools. Even after the Supreme Court declared segregation in public schools unconstitutional in its 1954 Brown *v.* Board of Education *decision, Mary chose to work in inner-city schools where students were mostly African Americans.*

family moved upstate to Idamay, West Virginia. There Mary continued her school and church activities. She attended Paul Lawrence Dunbar High School in nearby Fairmont. She taught children's Sunday School classes and sang in the church choir.

Tragedy Strikes

Mary and the McAdorys lived in Idamay until another tragedy struck the family in 1935. Aunt Booby went blind. The doctors said that she needed special medical care which she could not get in Idamay. So Mary moved again. This time the family went to live in Baltimore, Maryland. Mary would call this city "home" for the rest of her life.

The move to Baltimore brought great happiness to the McAdorys.[6] Doctors at Johns Hopkins Hospital saved Aunt Booby from her blindness. She could see again.[7] Mary was happy for her aunt. But she silently wished she were back in Idamay.[8] Mary felt that the people in the big city weren't very friendly.[9] And compared to her old school, the new school was a giant! Hundreds of students pushed their way through the halls of Frederick Douglass High School.

Mary had finished tenth grade at her old school. She had earned good grades. But she had not taken some of the classes she needed to graduate from Douglass High. So she repeated the grade.

At Douglass High, some of Mary's classmates teased her about her "small-town" ways and her good grades. One day one of her worst taunters gestured hatefully at her. Mary's temper flared, and a fight began. Mary bit the other girl's lip!

Both girls were sent home for the rest of the day. The next day, a teacher told how she had seen the fight. Mary was allowed to return to classes. "I learned I had to control my temper," she later realized. "But those girls never bothered me again!"[10]

Mary sometimes walked the five miles to Douglass High. Other days, she rode the city bus with her friend Mary Sawyer (Jones). The girls would talk about the many books that they had read. They would also make plans to do things together on weekends.

The two Marys especially looked forward to going uptown to Baltimore's Royal Theatre.[11] There they often saw the husband-wife comedy team named Butterbeans and Susie. They also enjoyed listening to famous musicians of that time, such as Duke Ellington, Ella Fitzgerald, and Louie Armstrong.[12]

"We saw Dusty Fletcher perform 'Open the Door, Richard!' [a comedy routine] at the Royal," recalls Mary Sawyer Jones. "I saw Mary tell that very same story at Morgan State over fifty years later. I thought it was hilarious, and I was amazed how she could remember it word-for-word!"[13]

Mary joined the Apostolic Faith Church in Baltimore. There she learned that she must "speak in tongues" to show her faith. She remembers:

> A dear lady with unpleasant breath kept repeating 'Hallelujah' in my ear. I didn't feel any emotion. I just wanted that dear lady out of my face. So, I cried out some gibberish so they would think I was speaking in tongues.[14]

New Friends

Sixteen-year-old Mary left the Apostolic Faith Church. She joined new friends at Baltimore's Waters A.M.E. Church. New friendships, though, brought new challenges.

Mary's new friends were taking her places where she saw people drinking alcohol. Leaders in the church taught that drinking alcohol was a sin. It was also illegal. "I wondered what was right and what was wrong," Mary wrote many years later.[15]

During her high school years, Mary worked as a "domestic" after school and during the summers. She cleaned people's houses, and washed and ironed their clothes. The work gave her street-car fare and "pocket money." It also helped her think about her future.

One day her boss ordered her to serve a glass of water. Mary laid aside her floor-scrubbing tools and stood up to obey. She remembers thinking, "I will *not* do this all my life!"[16]

Another time Mary's work made her think of Miss Gilbert's words years earlier.[17] Her employer had handed her a pair of dirty underpants to wash. Mary remembers scrubbing and thinking. She was thinking that one day she would, indeed, become the "Somebody" Miss Gilbert had talked about long ago.[18]

MILESTONES

Mary Rogers, be smart ! And stay in school ![1]

—Mary Deas "Mama" Nowden

Mary had learned many lessons from her grandmother. Mama Nowden had sparked her interest in stories, books, and songs. Mama Nowden had encouraged Mary to learn.

Mary graduated from Frederick Douglass High School in 1938. Her good grades showed that she had learned well. They also earned her the chance to learn more. She was awarded a free college education at Coppin Teachers College in Baltimore.*

* In 1950, Coppin Teachers College became Coppin State Teachers College. Then, in 1963, the name changed to Coppin State College.

Mary Rogers Coleman graduated from Frederick Douglass High School in Baltimore, Maryland.

Going to College

For as long as she could remember, Mary had dreamed of becoming a teacher.[2] Now she was the first person in her family to go to college. She was on her way to making her dream come true!

While in college, she lived at home with the McAdorys. She worked as a domestic for a while. Later she became one of the first African-American typists to work at Baltimore's Social Security office.

In her free time Mary went to every concert and show she could. Sometimes friends would take her backstage at the theater to meet performers she admired. Mary studied each famous person's style on stage. She also read about their lives.

One time she went to a concert by Billie Holiday. The blues singer always wore a flower in her hair. Mary read about Holiday. She learned that while the singer was getting ready for one of her concerts, her curling iron had become too hot. It burned off a piece of her hair. Holiday had quickly covered the bare spot with a gardenia. Even after her hair grew back, she continued to wear the flower.

Becoming a Teacher

Mary graduated from Coppin Teachers College in the spring of 1942. Then she began her first career. For thirty-one years, she would be an elementary school teacher and librarian in Baltimore's inner-city schools.

Four years into her teaching career, Mary met and fell in love with Ulysses J. Carter. The couple dated for only a short time. When they were married in 1946, Mary became known as Mary Coleman Carter.

Motherhood

Mary left teaching briefly when her only child Ricardo Rogers Carter was born on February 17, 1948. She loved being a mother.[3] She once wrote, "The sweetest sound I heard today . . . was the laughter of my child at play."[4]

Mary and her husband divorced after less than five years of marriage. She explains why she felt responsible for the divorce. "I didn't know marriage took hard work. I was a reader, a believer in fairy tales, in 'living happily ever after.'"[5]

When Ricky was a toddler, Mary returned to teaching. Leaving her son all day was not easy.[6]

Aunt Booby celebrated her niece's marriage to Ulysses J. Carter.

So she often took him with her to school activities. Ricky spent time with his mother's students. They came to his house for cookouts. He also went along with his mother when she did volunteer work at Maryland's School for the Blind.

Mary and her son spent time together at church activities. They went on picnics, took boat rides, and went to parks. They also went to baseball games and the zoo. In the summers the two of them visited Mary's uncle in New York.

Mary had always chosen to live in the inner-city. She explains:

> I wanted to stay and work with our children . . . I felt that I knew and understood black children, their problems and their needs. I wanted them to overcome their mistrust and hatred of the white world, to share my love and appreciation for the richness of our black heritage, to learn to be black and live black—without hating.[7]

As a single parent, Mary worried about raising her son in the inner-city.[8] Violence seemed to be everywhere. But her aunts and their families were now also living in Baltimore's inner-city. So Mary and her son stayed close to family.

Ricky often spent time with his father, Ulysses, and his half-brothers and sisters. Ulysses's death

Ricky Carter plays with his Cocker Spaniel named Frisky.

in 1960 was hard for twelve-year-old Ricky.[9] But during the same year a new family member came to live with him and his mother.

Mary had dated Elias Raymond Smith back in Idamay, West Virginia. When she learned that Elias's wife had died, she wrote her old boyfriend a letter. Soon, their friendship grew to love. They married, and Mary became known as Mary Carter Smith.

Happiness with her new husband was brief. Elias became very ill. Within two years after her wedding, Mary Carter Smith became a widow. Elias Raymond Smith died of kidney failure.

At the age of forty-three, Mary Carter Smith once again found herself grieving. Still she was not alone in the world. She had her faith in God. She had her son. She had her aunts and their families. And she had her students.

LIVING THE DREAM

If ever I have seen God, it's in the eyes of children.[1]

—Mary Carter Smith

"I always taught them that they were beautiful . . . and I read to them at the end of every day," Mary Carter Smith says about her work with thousands of students. "I was strict, but they knew I loved them!"[2]

For Mary Carter Smith, teaching was more than just giving lessons. She set out to encourage, support, and love each and every child.[3] Sometimes that meant writing a special book for a student who couldn't read. Other times it meant staying hours after school or visiting students' homes to share good news.

Learning about Africa

There weren't many books or stories about African-American people in the 1940s and 1950s. But Mary Carter Smith saw to it that her fourth and sixth graders learned about their roots.[4] She taught them African dances. She sang special religious songs called "Negro spirituals." She read and told all kinds of stories about Africa's people and their history.

Students in her class learned about Africa in other ways too. Their teacher dressed in African clothing. She wore loose-fitting pullover shirts called *dashikis* (də-shĕ́-kēz). She wore colorful necklaces and bracelets. And she wore head wraps called *geelees* (gā́-lēēz). She also helped the children cook African dishes.

Some of the other teachers seemed to think Mary Carter Smith's "Africa-talk" was silly. "'All she knows is Africa, Africa, Africa!'" she remembers them saying. "They used to laugh at me! But when Africa became popular, they stopped laughing!"[5]

Other teachers liked how she used African stories, art, foods, and clothing to help students learn about their roots.[6] "Mary was out on the cutting edge. I was amazed at what she could do with a story," exclaims former principal Dr. Rebecca Evans Carroll.[7] A past student, Wendell Green, remembers how Mary Carter Smith "wore the African attire [clothes] and was always dressed so brilliantly! She told stories as if she had been Native African, Native American, and Native European all rolled up together."[8]

Learning and Sharing

Mary Carter Smith had been writing poems and stories from the time she was in high school. "I was a good speller," she remembers. "But I didn't know all the rules of grammar."[9] So she took a college writing course. In the class she confessed her lack of grammar skills. The professor told her to just write the words and let editors worry about the correct grammar. "That freed me to write more."[10]

As usual, Mary Carter Smith taught her students what she'd learned. One time, a lesson of hers about writing proved very helpful to her students and to herself as well.

Say What You Think, Then Write It

She had encouraged her students to *say* what they were thinking and then *write* it. When President John F. Kennedy was shot and killed on November 22, 1963, Mary Carter Smith and her students talked about their sad feelings. Then they wrote their words as poems.

Mary Carter Smith loved to write letters.[11] She helped her students write letters to famous African Americans.[12] Poet and author Langston Hughes answered the children's letters. He also sent along some of his unpublished poems and folk tales. Langston Hughes and Mary Carter Smith wrote letters to each other for the next twenty years. "He always wrote in green ink!" she recalls about her friend.[13]

Pen Pal Langston Hughes

In the early 1950s Mary Carter Smith's students got to share the stage with their pen pal. Langston Hughes spoke at Coppin State Teachers College.

And the children's verse-speaking choir performed some of his poetry.

While in Baltimore, Mr. Hughes also saw Mary Carter Smith perform some of his work. Several years later, in 1967, he was planning to see her act in another one of his plays. But the sixty-five-year-old author and poet became ill. He died before he could return to Baltimore.

Mary Carter Smith recalls talking with Langston Hughes shortly before his death. "He told me he was afraid of doctors . . . he went to the hospital too late."[14]

As a college student and teacher, Mary Carter Smith had often volunteered her storytelling talents. She quickly became known around Baltimore. People liked her funny stories and monologues—the longer one-woman stories she presented.[15]

One of Mary Carter Smith's dreams had already come true. She had become a teacher. So when her son graduated and left home, she began to work toward another dream. But this dream was an expensive one! She wanted to take a trip to Africa.[16]

Visiting Africa

In 1969 Mary Carter Smith decided to make her dream come true.[17] She had to borrow the money to travel. A bank agreed to loan her the money, but she had to repay it. If she didn't, the bank would take her home from her.[18]

Friends had shared the names and addresses of people in Africa. So Mary wrote many letters before her trip. When she arrived in Liberia, whole families came from miles around to hear Mary Carter Smith, the African-American storyteller, tell her tales.

On her return to the United States, Mary Carter Smith had exciting new stories to tell. She had new ideas to write about. She also had a debt to pay. But she had visited Africa—her dream had come true!

Another important event happened in Mary Carter Smith's life in 1969. She and her cousin Joan Simmons Stephenson attended a poetry reading. During the evening they learned that the woman on stage had been paid for reading poems.[19] They also learned that the woman had an agent who scheduled readings for her.

That very night Mary Carter Smith got an idea. She wondered if people might pay to hear *her* perform.[20] The next morning, she called the woman's agent with a question. She wanted to know if the agent could schedule some readings for her, too.[21]

At first the agent didn't seem to be interested. Later he called with a problem. His usual performer would not be able to read poems for an audience in Augusta, Georgia. He asked if Mary Carter Smith could fill in!

"I got roses at intermission!" she beams. "They had my picture all around the hall. I was in seventh heaven!"[22] The agent called Mary Carter Smith with more requests to perform. Soon people were even calling her directly. "I learned that I didn't need an agent. I could book my own appearances!"[23] So she did.

Storytelling

Now she was telling stories to children five days a week in school. On the weekends she was telling stories to adults and children. Groups all over the South invited her to perform. Each time she told stories, Mary Carter Smith danced and sang. She also shared her message of peace and goodwill among people.

Mary Carter Smith on stage at the Arena Theatre in Baltimore.

"Being able to perform was like a fish finding water!" she exclaims.[24] She says she could tell stories for twelve hours without stopping! She adds that she never memorizes stories, except for Hans Christian Andersen's fables. "They're sooooo perfect."[25]

Mary Carter Smith had been telling stories and singing and dancing all her life. But now she was getting paid for performing! The extra income helped her repay the money she'd borrowed for her trip to Africa.

One night in 1971, she returned from a performance in Virginia. She felt happy and confident.[26] She felt that she had "built some bridges" with her stories and songs.[27] But the evening news upset her.[28]

There had been rioting among a young crowd at a Baltimore concert:

> The violence touched and troubled me. I saw the hatred, the misunderstanding, the frustration etched on the people's faces, and I didn't sleep that night. I felt God's call to be His messenger of peace and justice.[29]

The very next morning Mary Carter Smith asked for a leave from her job. She earned a leave because of her many years with the Baltimore schools. She could take a year off but still be paid half of her teaching salary. A year off meant that she could spend all her time telling stories. She could reach out and share her message of understanding and goodwill.

During the year's leave, Mary Carter Smith volunteered to tell stories wherever she was invited. She told stories in churches, prisons, Air Force bases, and schools. "I was invited to all-black schools, to all-white schools, and to integrated schools. In all of them, I felt good things happening [when I performed]."[30] She also traveled. It had been almost two years since her first trip to Africa. Now, she was going again!

Second Trip to Africa

Mary Carter Smith visited the nations of Ghana, Senegal, and Liberia. She wanted to learn more about each country's history and culture.[31] So she carefully planned her time. Once, she had to explain to her Liberian hosts why she couldn't spend more time visiting with important people:

> This is my homeland. I have been longing to visit here. Now my dream has come true. But look, I can't learn your culture if I visit the big shots. I have been visiting the average people, especially the children.[32]

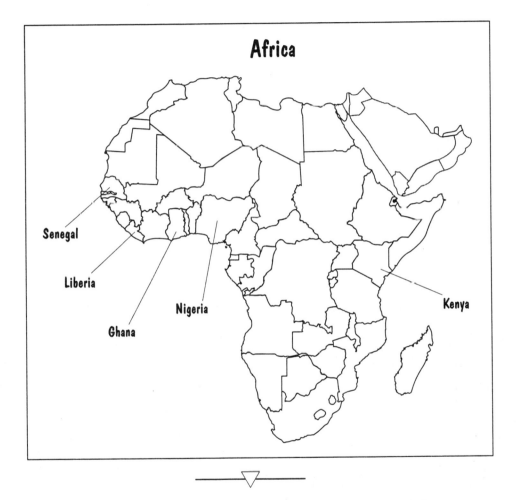

Africa

Senegal

Liberia

Nigeria

Ghana

Kenya

Mary Carter Smith made seven trips to Africa. She visited the nations of Nigeria, Ghana, Senegal, Kenya, and Liberia.

On her second visit to Africa, Mary Carter Smith took some surprises with her. She knew that people in Africa could not get things such as records by popular African-American musicians.[33] When people in Liberia came to hear her tell stories, their surprise was a copy of the hit record "Killing Me Softly," by Roberta Flack.

When her year's leave ended, Mary Carter Smith returned to her job as a school librarian. She still traveled and performed on the weekends. But by 1973 Mary Carter Smith knew she had to make a choice.[34] She could not continue her job *and* keep up with her storytelling.

After thirty-one years in the Baltimore schools, Mary Carter Smith retired. "It was such a sad day for the entire school," remembers past student Wendell Green.[35]

"Retirement" for Mary Carter Smith did not mean she would put her feet up and relax. Instead she devoted all her time to a new career.

"MY AMERICAN GRIOT"

When Mary Carter Smith tells a story, it's as if no one else is in the room but you.[1]

—Tina Hilton, journalist

"I don't expect you to believe my story, but tomorrow I die."[2] Mary Carter Smith grabbed the attention of nearly everyone in the room. More than six-hundred listeners at the 1987 Maryland Storytelling Festival sat on the edges of their seats. They waited to hear more. Mary Carter Smith gave them just that—a spine-tingling version of Edgar Allan Poe's "The Black Cat."

Mary Carter Smith often waves a switch when she tells stories! This is not a twig from a tree. It is a cowtail switch that has colorful beads on it. She brought it back from one of her seven trips to Africa. She explains that the beaded cowtail switch is a symbol of royalty in West Africa.

Becoming an Author

Along with stories, songs, and dancing, Mary Carter Smith's performances include some of her own writing. Ideas for her poems, stories, and essays come from her own joyful experiences and from painful ones too.

At first the storyteller wrote only for herself. She worried about what others might think of her writing.[3] But in 1966, Mary Carter Smith began to publish her poetry. *Town Child* and *Laugh a Little, Cry a Lot* are two books of her original poems.

She has also published other kinds of writing. In 1985 she and two friends co-authored *The Griots' Cookbook: Rare and Well-Done*. The book is full of down-home recipes sprinkled with bits of poetry. Mary Carter Smith also wrote a travel series for Baltimore's *Afro-American* newspaper. The series of articles came from the diary she kept during her visits to Africa.

Mary Carter Smith has published her writing for the same reasons she performs as a storyteller. She has tried to:

> . . . foster better human relations. I am against war. . . . I am for love and brotherhood. . . . I am an activist for the rights of all people, whatever their color, sex, ethnic origin, or age.[4]

The storytelling author traveled all over the world. People of all ages, races, and religions came to hear her tell stories. *Wall Street Journal* writer Leon E. Wynter told his readers:

> Ms. Smith spins her tales with a gossipy style that suggests she is leaning over a backyard fence talking with a neighbor . . . [she] is helping to carry on the rich tradition of black storytelling.[5]

Learning about Herself

Even as a five-year-old, Mary Carter Smith had been able to tell a story that made people listen. Her grandmother had not approved of the stories she told on the street long ago. Mama Nowden, though, would have been proud of her granddaughter now. Mama Nowden would have been pleased with Mary Carter Smith's life work—to encourage peace and justice.[6]

Mary Carter Smith knew that her roots were in Africa.[7] She had learned this long ago on Mama Nowden's lap. But as an adult, she read a book that taught her more about herself. She learned that her special kind of storytelling also had its roots in Africa.[8]

The book, *From Slavery to Freedom, A History of Negro Americans*, told about *griots* (grēē′-ōz). The authors said that griots in Africa were like "living dictionaries." African griots remembered the ancestors, or people who had lived long ago. The griots told about those people's lives. They told all this history through songs, stories, and poetry.[9] The book also said that griots had performed for African kings as early as 1500 A.D. "It amazed me that the thing I had been doing all my life had an African name!" Mary Carter Smith once wrote.[10]

In 1975 she learned still more about her storytelling's roots from a good friend. At the time, she was a member of a planning board at Orchard Street Church. The old church needed some repairs. So the committee was

Mary Carter Smith is shown here in her first professional photo taken in 1973.

planning an event to raise money. James Walker of the National Archives in Washington, D.C., had been invited to speak. Mary Carter Smith would tell stories.

A Very Special Guest Speaker

The church members also wanted to invite Alex Haley to speak.[11] Mr. Haley had edited Malcolm X's autobiography in 1965. Since then he had been finding out and writing about his own African heritage. Bernice Takach asked if anyone knew Alex Haley. Mary Carter Smith said that she'd just mailed him a birthday cake!

Ms. Takach then wrote to Alex Haley. She asked if he would speak at the church event. In a letter dated July 19, 1975, Alex Haley wrote:

> In response, I put it this way, such is my respect for James Walker and Mary Carter Smith that you can be certain that I go way out of my way to share appearance on a program with them [sic] . . . the main problem being that the filming of my coming book *Roots* (to be published next March) will start during October and will probably continue into February, with me very much involved in the production.[12]

On October 9 Alex Haley wrote again:

> I am deep into finishing the book on which I have been working for 10 years, . . . It's cute, your account of how you met Mary Carter Smith and asked if she knew me, to learn that she just mailed me a cake. Have you ever tasted Mary Carter Smith's coconut pound cake? If you haven't, you've missed something.[13]

In her own letters to Alex Haley, Mary Carter Smith kept her friend up-to-date on the plans. She sent along newspaper clippings about the event. One article said, "Alex Haley is one of the most famous of all living authors."[14]

"I dream like all writers that one day might be said [sic], but it's sure not now the case," Alex Haley wrote to Mary Carter Smith.[15] During that time he also wrote to Bernice Takach:

> To tell you the truth, sentimentally, I'll forever regard myself as a Tennessee boy who was raised by my dear, wise, good grandma and somehow I've never gotten very carried away with this so-called celebrity business.[16]

Less than a year later, even the "Tennessee boy" himself would have had to admit that he had become "one of the most famous of all living authors." In 1976 Alex Haley's new book *Roots: The Saga of a Family* became a best-seller. The next year Alex Haley won a Special Citation

*Mary Carter Smith and Bernice Takach welcomed author Alex
Haley to Baltimore.*

Pulitzer Prize. He also became famous for the television mini-series based on his book.

Mary Carter Smith remembers Alex Haley's visit to Baltimore:

> I prepared dinner for him in my home and we talked. He told me it was through an African griot that he was able to make the connection between the stories his aunts had told him of his ancestor Kunta Kinte and Africa. The griot remembered Kunta Kinte.[17]

Mary Carter Smith remembers how Alex Haley honored her that evening. "He called me 'My American Griot.'"[18]

REACHING OUT

She's a boundless source of energy and love ![1]

—Reverend P. M. Smith

"Mary Carter Smith is powerful! Most people see a situation and go away from it. Mary will see a situation and go *toward* it," says school social worker and friend Wilnetta Sutton.[2] Over the years Mary Carter Smith has faced many challenges head-on. She saw all kinds of people who needed her help.

Seven-year-old Angie was often "in trouble" at school. So her neighbor, Mary Carter Smith, made time to be with Angie. "I just loved her!

She needed somebody."[3] Eleven-year-old Cynthia couldn't live with her family anymore. So Mary Carter Smith found the girl a safe loving home. Another child's home was destroyed by fire. So Mary Carter Smith helped gather clothing for the girl and her family.

Mary Carter Smith was there for hundreds of other girls. She led Girl Scout troops. She organized Good News Clubs. The clubs met once a week after school to read the Bible and perform Biblical stories.

But more and more children needed help. There seemed to be so many young black girls who needed caring adult women in their lives. Mary Carter Smith decided to do something to help.[4] She talked with a friend. The two of them made a plan.[5]

A Plan that Grew and Grew

They collected names of people who wanted to help. They worked to raise money. And in 1965 Sedonia Merritt and Mary Carter Smith co-founded the Baltimore Big Sister-Little Sister organization. Mary Carter Smith was the group's president for five years. She also had a Little

Sister of her own. For years Mary Carter Smith had been a role model for young girls. Now others were following her lead. Many Big Sisters spent time with Little Sisters.

The Big Sister-Little Sister group began in Baltimore's African-American community. Soon women of other races were helping. By 1994, the group had over one hundred active Big Sister-Little Sister matches. Later the Baltimore group became part of Big Brothers-Big Sisters of America. Mary Carter Smith was vice-president of its board of directors.

Touching More Lives

Mary Carter Smith reached out to touch the lives of still others. Yvette Thomas (Wellons) Hector remembers when Mary Carter Smith taught Vacation Bible School:

> She always welcomed us with a smile and open arms . . . to date most of us (the children of the church) are in touch with each other. We are because [Mary Carter Smith] took the time to nurture us. I remember the many evenings we went up to her house for refreshments and sat and listened to her recite, read, or sing.[6]

Yvette Hector also remembers her young friends telling stories from home. They said Mary Carter Smith had taken them to get new shoes. They said she had given their mothers rent money. They said she had brought their families coal to heat their houses.

Yvette Hector tells how Mary Carter Smith's kindness taught her to also help others. Ms. Hector's son had passed away. Mary Carter Smith gave her $200 for the burial. "I cried . . . Mary walked over to me, put her arm around me and said, 'little sister, I understand' . . . that one act of loving care changed me . . . and [since then] I have found joy in giving to others."[7]

Two Steps Towards Awareness

In 1981 Mary Carter Smith met another challenge head-on. Martin Luther King, Jr.'s birthday was already a holiday in Maryland and nine other states. Many Americans wanted the day to be a national holiday. People such as Mary Carter Smith helped to make it happen.

She organized a group of people in Baltimore. The group worked to tell others about Dr. King's life and his work. They planned special events for

January 15, Dr. King's birthday. The events were so successful that they were repeated the following years.[8] Then in 1992 the U.S. Congress made King's birthday a national holiday.

Mary Carter Smith met still another challenge in 1982. She was attending the Tenth Annual Festival of the National Storytelling Association. She and another storyteller saw something that day in Jonesborough, Tennessee.

"It was like a storybook town," Mary Carter Smith recalls, "but we saw very few black people there."[9] So she and Linda Goss began to work toward a dream. They wanted to begin a black storyteller's group.[10]

People seemed to like the idea. The next year Baltimore hosted the first festival of what would later be known as the National Association of Black Storytellers.

Mary Carter Smith has also reached out to others through radio and television. She was hostess for Maryland Public Television's "Black Is." She hosted "The Children's Hour" at a university's radio station in Washington, D.C.

But the storyteller wanted to reach the children in her own city of Baltimore.[11] So she volunteered to create and host her own radio program.

Baltimore listeners, young and old, have been tuning in to hear "Griot for the Young and Young at Heart" since 1977. Mary Carter Smith tells stories, recites poems, and sings songs. She also directs her child guests in on-the-air verse-speaking choirs.

A Terrible Tragedy

For many years, Mary Carter Smith has worked to help others. Once, she even helped someone who had hurt her very badly. Her only son, Ricardo Rogers Carter, had finished college. He hoped to teach art.[12] His mother was excited.[13] She wanted to see Ricky work with children.[14] She also wanted to see him as a husband and a father.[15] She remembered the times Mama Nowden had rocked her and told her stories. Now she dreamed of the day when *she* might rock and tell stories to her own grandchild.[16]

A moment of violence stole Mary Carter Smith's dreams. On January 6, 1978, twenty-nine-year-old Ricardo Rogers Carter lost his life in a Baltimore stabbing.

After his graduation from high school, Ricardo Rogers Carter studied art at Morgan State University in Baltimore.

Mary Carter Smith saw her son's murderer for the first time at the trial. "I was glad the woman was in custody. I wanted her to reap a portion of the hurt she had sown."[17] As the victim's mother watched, however, the woman didn't seem to care that she had taken the life of Ricardo Rogers Carter. Mary Carter Smith felt her hatred grow to rage.[18]

8

A Legacy

Treasures should be preserved.[1]

—R. B. Jones, journalist

Mary Carter Smith lost her only child. But hatred and rage did not stay in her heart.

> I realized that I couldn't call myself a Christian and hate the woman who had killed my son . . . I thought of her mother. I had lost a son, but she had a daughter who had taken somebody's life, and I went to where she lived and talked with her . . . she was hurting almost as badly as I.[2]

In June 1979 Ricardo Rogers Carter's murderer was found guilty. The woman was sentenced to ten years in prison. But Mary Carter

Smith had been sentenced to a lifetime of grieving for her son.

Forgiving

A year later Mary Carter Smith's faith was tested again:

> I was scheduled to speak at a pre-release center for women prisoners in Baltimore. When I called to confirm the engagement, the woman in charge said "I think I should tell you, Mrs. Smith, that the woman who killed your son is here."
>
> That rocked me. But I said I would go as planned. I spoke but I didn't see her among those gathered in the room. Afterward, I was told . . . she wanted to see me. She came downstairs and for half an hour we talked. I saw not the arrogant young woman I had remembered from the trial but a troubled human being asking for help—asking to be forgiven . . . though seeing her brought back a flood of unhappy memories, I forgave [her].[3]

Mary Carter Smith also helped her son's murderer. To get an early release, the woman had to have a job outside the prison. So Mary Carter Smith helped her find a job. "I write to her from time to time . . . I will do for her whatever she allows me to do. . . . At least she knows that she is forgiven."[4]

Over the years Mary Carter Smith has included stories about her son's life and death in some of her performances. When asked about her choice of stories for audiences, she once said, "I face the audience and feel their 'vibes' to decide what I will do."[5]

Sometimes she says she feels the "vibes" are right for sharing personal stories. She shares her childhood "naughties" and her years with Mama Nowden and Aunt Booby. She shares the time spent learning from the "greats" in the theaters and concert halls of Baltimore. She also shares with her audience the joyful and painful memories of mothering her child.[6]

Reverend P. M. Smith, pastor at Baltimore's Huber Memorial Church, says that Mary Carter Smith's story about losing her son is far-reaching:

> She uses that to minister to other people who have lost children . . . this lady who everybody recognizes is *special* . . . lets them know how *angry* she was and how she hated this person and how she cried night after night.[7]

Giving and Receiving

During her seventh decade, Mary Carter Smith began to slow down. She gave only one or two performances a month. But she still made time for the many special people in her life. Among those are her twelve godchildren—some young and others "young at heart."

Throughout her life, as a friend, parent, godparent, teacher, storyteller, folklorist, author, poet, actress, lecturer, social activist, radio-television personality, and world traveler, Mary Carter Smith has shared her talents and her love for all people. She has also received much love and respect in return.

For more than thirty years people have honored her. Mary Carter Smith became "Baltimore's Official Griot" in 1983. She became "Maryland's Official Griot" in 1991. In 1994 over 500 members of the National Association of Black Storytellers honored their group's co-founder. Mary Carter Smith was named "America's Mother Griot."

A wax statue of Mary Carter Smith can be seen at Baltimore's Great Blacks in Wax Museum. A limited edition of the "Mary Carter Smith Mother Griot" doll came out in 1994. All money from the doll's sales goes to the National Association of Black Storytellers.

In 1981, journalist and professor Dr. E. Lee Lassiter asked his readers to "do the

Mary Carter Smith waves her cowtail switch in one of her church performances.

Mary Carter Smith and friend Eugene Grove visit her wax likeness.

world a big favor by capturing Mary Carter Smith in her natural habitat and preserving her for posterity."[8] Since then Mary Carter Smith's storytelling performances have been preserved on cassettes. They are titled *Mary Carter Smith Presents, Mary Carter Smith: Nearing Seventy-five, Tell Me a Story,* and *Cindy Ellie.*

Encouraging Others

Mary Carter Smith once said, "When a griot dies, it's as though a library has burned down."[9] She believes that there must always be griots to tell the stories of Africa.[10] This is why she encourages other storytellers. She is a founding member of the Griots' Circle of Maryland.

Mary Carter Smith has also worked hard to train young storytellers. In 1993 the radio station WEAA-FM of Baltimore and local store owners founded the "Growing Griots" club. Soon more than fifty storytellers, ages five through thirteen, had joined Mary Carter Smith. Ten-year-old Miracle Banks became one of the first members of "Growing Griots." This young griot-in-training was *born* with a story to tell!

Miracle Banks kicked and screamed her way into the world on January 17, 1983. She weighed less than one and one-half pounds. Feeling blessed, Richard and Yvonne Banks wanted to give their tiny daughter an African name that meant "miracle."[11] So they talked to Mary Carter Smith, the griot they'd heard on WEAA-FM radio.

There didn't seem to be an African name. So the Banks named their tiny baby "Miracle." And the family's new griot friend "adopted" Miracle as her all-time-smallest-ever godchild.

For more than seventy-five years, Mary Carter Smith has been touching the lives of millions of people. Storytelling has been one of her most powerful tools. When asked about her goals for the future, she says, "I am among those who fight misunderstanding.

This 1973 photograph of Mary Carter Smith shows her early in her storytelling career. She has come full circle with her efforts to train up-and-coming young storytellers.

The weapons I use are stories, drama, songs, poetry, and laughter . . . my mission is to leave a measure of peace and understanding in the world."[12]

CHRONOLOGY

1919—On February 10, Mary Rogers Ward is born in Birmingham, Alabama.

1923—Mary's mother Eartha Nowden marries Warren Coleman. Mary becomes known as Mary Rogers Coleman.

1924—Mary's mother is murdered by new husband Earl Knight in New York City.

1932—Mary's grandmother Mary Deas "Mama" Nowden dies of cancer.

1935—Mary moves to Baltimore with Aunt Booby and Uncle Norman McAdory.

1942—Mary graduates from Coppin Teachers College. She begins her thirty-one-year career as school teacher and librarian in Baltimore's elementary schools.

1946—Mary marries Ulysses J. Carter and becomes known as Mary Coleman Carter. The couple divorces within five years.

1948—Mary's only child Ricardo Rogers Carter is born.

1960—Mary marries childhood friend Elias Raymond Smith. She becomes known as Mary Carter Smith. She is widowed in less than two years of marriage when Elias dies of kidney failure.

1965—Mary and Sedonia Merritt co-found Baltimore's Big Sister-Little Sister chapter.

1969—Mary gives her first paid storytelling performance. She visits Ghana during first trip to Africa.

1971—Mary takes a year's leave from Baltimore schools to volunteer storytelling performances. She visits Ghana, Senegal, and Liberia in Africa, and performs in France.

1973—Mary retires from Baltimore Schools. She becomes a full-time storyteller and visits Africa twice.

1974—Mary visits Ghana.

1975—Mary begins long career as volunteer creator, producer, and host of Morgan State University's WEAA-FM radio program, *Griot for the Young and Young at Heart*, in Baltimore.

1978—Mary visits England and Nigeria. She performs in the Caribbean. Ricardo Rogers Carter is murdered in a Baltimore stabbing.

1979—Mary visits Kenya and Paris, France.

1981—Mary is founder and president of Citizen's Coalition of Baltimore. She organizes events to encourage national observance of Martin Luther King, Jr.'s birthday.

1982—Mary visits Haiti.

1983—Mary is honored as "Baltimore's Official Griot." Mary and storyteller Linda Goss co-found National Association of Black Storytellers.

1984—Mary visits Nigeria.

1988—Mary performs in the Caribbean.

1989—Mary's likeness is installed in Baltimore's Great Blacks in Wax Museum.

1991—Mary is honored as "Maryland's Official Griot."

1993—Mary trains young storytellers in WEAA-FM's "Growing Griots" club.

1994—Mary is proclaimed "America's Mother Griot" by National Association of Black Storytellers. A limited-edition of "Mary Carter Smith Mother Griot" doll is introduced.

CHAPTER NOTES

Chapter 1

1. Seymour Kopf referring to Mary Carter Smith, "Man About Town," *The News American* (Baltimore), October 18, 1972.

2. Personal interview with Mary Carter Smith, February 18, 1994; Mary Carter Smith, "Christ and a Griot," unpublished, 1993, p. 3.

3. Ibid.

4. Ibid.

5. Ibid.

6. Telephone interview with Mary Carter Smith, February 8, 1994; Mary Carter Smith, "Christ and a Griot,"p. 3.

7. Ibid.

8. Personal interview; Jimmy Neil Smith, *Homespun Tales from America's Favorite Storytellers* (New York: Crown Publishers, Inc., 1988), p. 174.

9. Jimmy Neil Smith, p. 174.

10. Mary Carter Smith,"Christ and a Griot," p. 3.

11. Personal interview.

12. Mary Deas "Mama" Nowden as quoted by Mary Carter Smith, "Christ and a Griot," p. 3.

13. Mary Carter Smith as quoted by Larry Pike, "Profiles: A Modern Griot," *Storytelling Magazine*, Summer 1993, pp. 28.

Chapter 2

1. Mary Carter Smith as quoted by Jimmy Neil Smith, *Homespun Tales from America's Favorite Storytellers* (New York: Crown Publishers, Inc., 1988), p. 173.

2. Personal interview with Mary Carter Smith, February 18, 1994.

3. Ibid.; "Myself, My Roots, June 1980," in Mary Carter Smith, *Heart to Heart* (Baltimore: Aframa Agency, 1988), pp. 168–169.

4. Ibid., p. 168.

5. Personal interview; Jimmy Neil Smith, p. 172.

6. Mary Carter Smith, "Christ and a Griot," unpublished, 1993, p. 2.

7. Personal interview; Jimmy Neil Smith, p. 173.

8. Telephone interview with Mary Carter Smith, March 7, 1994.

9. Ibid.

10. Ibid.

11. Leon E. Wynter, "Tale of Cindy Ellie, Voodoo Godmother And White Cadillac: Black Storytellers Carry On A Rich, Tribal Tradition; Break-Dancing Butterfly," *The Wall Street Journal,* January 22, 1990; personal interview.

12. Telephone interview with Mary Carter Smith, March 7, 1994.

13. Ibid.

14. Mary Carter Smith, "Christ and a Griot," p. 1.

15. Personal interview; Jimmy Neil Smith p. 173.

16. Telephone interview with Mary Carter Smith, March 7, 1994.

17. Mary Carter Smith, "Christ and a Griot," p. 3.

18. Editorial, "Women's World: Keeping Black Heritage Alive," *The News American* (Baltimore), December 13, 1974.

19. Mary Carter Smith, "Christ and a Griot," p.1.

20. Telephone interview with Mary Carter Smith, March 7, 1994; Jimmy Neil Smith, p. 173.

21. Telephone interview with Mary Carter Smith, March 7, 1994.

22. Personal interview with Mary Carter Smith, March 7, 1994; Mary Carter Smith "Christ and a Griot," p. 2.

23. Ibid.

24. Ibid.

25. Mary Carter Smith, "Christ and a Griot," p. 4; Mary Carter Smith, "Myself, My Roots," p. 169.

26. Ibid.

27. Telephone interview with Mary Carter Smith, March 7, 1994.

28. Personal interview.

29. Jimmy Neil Smith, p. 174; Mary Carter Smith, "Christ and a Griot," p. 4.

30. Mary Carter Smith, "Myself, My Roots," p. 170.

31. Elder Witt, *Guide to the United States Supreme Court*, 2nd ed., (Washington, D.C.: Congressional Quarterly Inc., 1990), pp. 39–40, 338, 901.

32. Telephone interview with Mary Carter Smith, March, 7, 1994; telephone interview with Marie Howard Adams, June 1, 1994.

33. Mary Carter Smith, "Myself, My Roots," p. 169.

34. Personal interview; Mary Carter Smith, "Christ and a Griot," p. 5.

35. Ibid.

36. Mary Carter Smith, "Christ and a Griot,"p. 5.

37. Telephone interview with Mary Carter Smith, March, 7, 1994.

38. Ibid.

Chapter 3

1. Telephone interview with Mary Sawyer Jones, March 7, 1994.

2. Elder Witt, *Guide to the United States Supreme Court*, 2nd ed., (Washington, D.C.: Congressional Quarterly Inc., 1990), pp. 48–49, 909.

3. Mary Carter Smith, "Christ and a Griot," unpublished, 1993, p. 5; Mary Carter Smith, "Myself, My Roots, June 1980," in Mary Carter Smith, *Heart to Heart* (Baltimore: Aframa Agency, 1988), p. 170

4. Witt, pp. 48-49, 909.

5. Dr. Frances Beckles, *20 Black Women* (Baltimore: Gateway Press, Inc., 1978), p. 108.

6. Telephone interview with Mary Carter Smith, March 13, 1994.

7. Ibid.

8. Ibid.

9. Ibid.

10. Telephone interview with Mary Carter Smith, March 23, 1994.

11. Telephone interview with Mary Sawyer Jones, March, 7, 1994.

12. Ibid.

13. Ibid.

14. Mary Carter Smith, "Christ and a Griot," p. 6.

15. Ibid.

16. Telephone interview with Mary Carter Smith, March 13, 1994.

17. Ibid.

18. Ibid.

Chapter 4

1. Mary Deas "Mama" Nowden as quoted by Mary Carter Smith, telephone interview, March 13, 1994.

2. Mary Carter Smith notes, March 14, 1994.

3. Telephone interview with Mary Carter Smith, April 13, 1994.

4. Mary Carter Smith, "Memorabilia," in Mary Carter Smith, *Heart to Heart* (Baltimore, Maryland: Aframa Agency, 1988), p. 180.

5. Mary Carter Smith, "Christ and a Griot," unpublished, 1993, p. 6.

6. Telephone interview with Mary Carter Smith, April 13, 1994.

7. Mary Carter Smith as quoted by Larry Pike, "Profiles: A Modern Griot," *Storytelling Magazine*, Summer 1993, p. 28; Mary Carter Smith as quoted by Jimmy Neil Smith, *Homespun Tales from America's Favorite Storytellers* (New York: Crown Publishers, Inc. 1988), p. 174.

8. Mary Carter Smith, "Ricky," in Mary Carter Smith, *Heart to Heart* (Baltimore, Maryland: Aframa Agency, 1988), p. 154.

9. Telephone interview with Mary Carter Smith, April 13, 1994.

Chapter 5

1. Mary Carter Smith as quoted by Joyce Muller, "Storytellers Hold Forth from the Hilltop," *The Hill: Western Maryland College*, August 1987.

2. Personal interview with Mary Carter Smith, February 18, 1994.

3. Ibid.

4. Helen R. Brown, "Her Career Adds Up To a Children's Story," *The News American* (Baltimore), February 9, 1973, p. 13-A.

5. Personal interview; Larry Pike, "Profiles: A Modern Griot," *Storytelling Magazine*, Summer 1993, p. 28.

6. Personal interview.

7. Telephone interview with Dr. Rebecca Evans Carroll, March 14, 1994.

8. Telephone interview with Wendell Green, March 18, 1994.

9. Telephone interview with Mary Carter Smith, March 7, 1994.

10. Ibid.

11. Personal interview.

12. Ibid.

13. Ibid.

14. Ibid.

15. Ibid.

16. Telephone interview with Mary Carter Smith, April 13, 1994.

17. Mary Carter Smith, "Declaration," *SCOPE*, November 1971, p. 15; personal interview.

18. Ibid.

19. Mary Carter Smith as quoted by Larry Pike.

20. Ibid.; personal interview.

21. Ibid.

22. Ibid.

23. Personal interview.

24. Ibid.; Mary Carter Smith as quoted in editorial, "Keeping Black Heritage Alive," *The News American* (Baltimore), December 13, 1974.

25. Mary Carter Smith as quoted by Joyce Muller.

26. Mary Carter Smith as quoted by Jimmy Neil Smith, *Homespun Tales from America's Favorite Storytellers* (New York: Crown Publishers, Inc., 1988), p. 175.

27. Ibid.

28. Ibid., p. 174.

29. Ibid.

30. Mary Carter Smith, "The Risk in Forgiving," *Faith at Work*, November/December 1990, p. 14.

31. Personal interview.

32. Mary Carter Smith as quoted by Jack Blamo Robinson, "Afro-American TV Star Here to Study Liberian Folklore," *The Liberian Age* (Liberia, Africa), January 23, 1970.

33. Personal interview.

34. Ibid.; Dr. Frances Beckles, *20 Black Women* (Baltimore: Gateway Press, Inc., 1978), p. 111.

35. Telephone interview with Wendell Green.

Chapter 6

1. Tina Hilton, "Woman spellbinds crowds with her storytelling magic," *Johnson City Press* (Johnson City, Tennessee), October 6, 1985.

2. Mary Carter Smith, "The Risk in Forgiving," *Faith at Work*, November/December 1990, p. 14; Mary Carter Smith as quoted by Joyce Muller, "Storytellers Hold Forth from the Hilltop," *The Hill: Western Maryland College*, August 1987.

3. Telephone interview with Mary Carter Smith, April 13, 1994.

4. Mary Carter Smith as quoted by Helen R. Brown "Her Career Adds Up To a Children's Story," *The News American* (Baltimore), February 9, 1973, p.13-A; Mary Carter Smith as quoted by Joyce Muller.

5. Leon E. Wynter, "Tale of Cindy Ellie, Voodoo Godmother And White Cadillac: Black Storytellers Carry On A Rich, Tribal Tradition; Break-Dancing Butterfly," *The Wall Street Journal*, January 22, 1990.

6. Joyce Muller.

7. Personal interview with Mary Carter Smith, February 18, 1994.

8. Ibid.; Mary Carter Smith, "Christ and a Griot," unpublished, 1993, p. 9.

9. John Hope Franklin and Alfred A. Moss, Jr., *From Slavery to Freedom: A History of Negro Americans* (New York: McGraw-Hill Publishing Company), Sixth Edition, 1988, p. 23.

10. Mary Carter Smith, "Christ and a Griot." p. 9.

11. Personal interview.

12. Alex Haley, letter dated July 19, 1975, as included in Elizabeth M. Oliver, "Haley came in 1975 to honor our roots in Orchard Church," *Baltimore Afro-American*, February 5, 1977.

13. Alex Haley, letter dated October 9, 1975, as included in Elizabeth M. Oliver.

14. Quote from newspaper clipping as quoted by Alex Haley in his letter to Mary Carter Smith, included in Elizabeth M. Oliver.

15. Alex Haley, letter to Mary Carter Smith as included in Elizabeth M. Oliver.

16. Alex Haley, letter to Bernice Takach dated October 9, 1975, as included in Elizabeth M. Oliver.

17. Personal interview; Mary Carter Smith, "Christ and a Griot," p. 9.

18. Ibid.

Chapter 7

1. Telephone interview with Reverend P. M. Smith, May 25, 1994.

2. Telephone interview with Wilnetta and Clearman Sutton, March 17, 1994.

3. Personal interview with Mary Carter Smith, February 18, 1994.

4. Wilnetta and Clearman Sutton.

5. Ibid.

6. Yvette Thomas (Wellons) Hector, letter to the author, April 12, 1994.

7. Ibid.

8. Ron Davis, "Spending boycott in support of national King holiday seems to work," *The Sun* (Baltimore), January 16, 1982; Lawrence Kessner, "Blacks urged to refrain from spending on King's birthday," *Evening Sun* (Baltimore), December 28, 1982.

9. Mary Carter Smith as quoted by Larry Pike, "Profiles: A Modern Griot," *Storytelling Magazine*, Summer 1993, p. 29.

10. Larry Pike; NABS brochure, "Brief History of the National Association of Black Storytellers, Inc."

11. Personal interview.

12. Telephone interview with Mary Carter Smith, June 2, 1994.

13. Ibid.

14. Ibid.

15. Ibid.

16. Ibid.

17. Mary Carter Smith, "Ricky," *Heart to Heart* (Baltimore: Aframa Agency, 1988), p. 154; "The Risk in Forgiving," *Faith at Work*, November/December, 1990, p. 13.

18. Mary Carter Smith, "The Risk in Forgiving," p. 12; Mary Carter Smith, "Ricky."

Chapter 8

1. R. B. Jones referring to Mary Carter Smith, "Mary Carter Smith's performance at Arena Players is priceless," *Baltimore Afro-American*, March 8, 1987.

2. Mary Carter Smith, "The Risk in Forgiving," *Faith at Work*, November/December 1990, p. 13.

3. Ibid., p. 14.

4. Ibid.

5. Mary Carter Smith as quoted by Joyce Muller, "Storytellers Hold Forth from the Hilltop," *The Hill: Western Maryland College*, August 1987.

6. Personal interview with Mary Carter Smith, February 18, 1994; Mary Carter Smith, "Legacy," radio program "Griot for the Young and Young at Heart," recorded at Morgan State University WEAA-FM radio, January 29, 1994.

7. Telephone interview with Reverend P. M. Smith, May 25, 1994.

8. E. Lee Lassiter, "Griot's concerts should be filmed," *The News* (Baltimore), December 7, 1981; telephone interview with Dr. E. Lee Lassiter, March 22, 1994.

9. Mary Carter Smith as quoted by Hariette Insignares, "From one Storyteller to another: A tribute to Mary Carter Smith," *Nashville Pride*, April 14, 1989.

10. Telephone interview with Mary Carter Smith, June 2, 1994.

11. Telephone interviews with Richard, Yvonne, and Miracle Banks, May 31, 1994.

12. Personal interview; Mary Carter Smith, "The Risk in Forgiving," p. 14; Joyce Muller.

FURTHER READING

Hamilton, Virginia. *The Magical Adventures of Pretty Pearl*. New York: Harper, 1983.

Haskins, James. *The Scottsboro Boys*. New York: Holt, 1993.

Hughes, Langston. *The First Book of Jazz*. 2nd ed. New York: Franklin Watts, 1976.

Lawler, Mary. *Black Americans of Achievement Series: Marcus Garvey*. New York: Chelsea House Publishers, 1988.

Rogers, Joel Augustus. *Your History: From the Beginning of Time to the Present*. 2nd ed. Baltimore: Black Classic Press, 1983.

Rowland, Della. *Martin Luther King Jr.: The Dream of a Peaceful Revolution*. Morristown, NJ: Silver Burdett Press, 1990.

Rummel, Jack. *Black Americans of Achievement Series: Langston Hughes*. New York: Chelsea House Publishers, 1988.

Smith, Mary Carter. *Town Child*, 4th ed. Baltimore: Aframa Agency, 1991.

Stewart, Gail B. *Timelines 1920's*. New York: Crestwood House, 1989.

———. *Timelines 1930's*. New York: Crestwood House, 1989.

Yarborough, Camille. *Cornrows*. New York: Putnam, 1979.

Further Viewing and Listening

Haley, Alex. *Roots*. Vol. I-VI, (videocasette). Burbank, CA: Warner Communications, 1977.

Smith, Mary Carter. "Cindy Ellie," *American Storytelling Series*, Vol. V, (videocasette). Bronx, NY: H. W. Wilson Co., 1986.

———. *Mary Carter Smith Presents*. (audiocasette). Baltimore: Aframa Agency, 1984.

———. *Tell Me a Story*. (videocassette). Irwindale, CA: Barr Entertainment, 1986.

BIBLIOGRAPHY

Goss, Linda, and Marian E. Barnes, ed. *Talk that Talk: An Anthology of African-American Storytelling*. New York: Simon & Schuster, 1989.

Haley, Alex. *Roots: The Saga of a Family*. New York: Doubleday, 1976.

Haley, Alex, and Malcolm X. *The Autobiography of Malcolm X*. New York: Ballantinc Books, 1992.

Hughes, Langston. *Five Plays*. Bloomington, IN: Indiana University Press, 1968.

Hughes, Langston, and Arna Bontemps, ed. *The Poetry of the Negro*. New York: Doubleday, 1970.

"Open the Door, Richard!" © 1980 Mary Carter Smith, unpublished.

Poe, Edgar Allan. *Complete Stories and Poems of Edgar Allan Poe*. New York: Doubleday & Co., 1966.

Smith, Mary Carter, Alice McGill, and Elmira M. Washington, *The Griots' Cookbook: Rare and Well-Done*. Columbia, MD: C. H. Fairfax Company, 1985.

Smith, Mary Carter, *A Few Words*. Baltimore: Aframa Agency, 1971.

———. *Laugh a Little, Cry a Lot*. Appalachia, VA: Young Publications, 1967.

———. *Mary Carter Smith ... Nearing Seventy-five*. (audiocassette). Baltimore: Aframa Agency, 1994.

———. *Opinionated*. Baltimore: Beacon Press, 1966.

———. *Vibes*. Columbia, MD.: Nordika Publications, 1974.

Other

National Association of Black Storytellers, Inc., P.O. Box 67722, Baltimore, MD 21215, Telephone (410) 947-1117.

National Storytelling Association, P.O. Box 309, Jonesborough, TN 37659, Telephone (615) 753-2171.

HONORS AND AWARDS

Sojourner Truth Award, 1965

Distinguished Alumni Citation, Coppin State College, 1966

Community Service Award, National Council of Jewish Women, 1967

Outstanding Soror Award (Philadelphia), 1967

Afro-American Newspaper Award, 1968

Distinguished Teacher Award, National Council of Negro Women, 1968

Fellowship, Juvenile Writer's Workshop, Temple Buell College, 1968

Fellowship, *Guidepost* Writers Workshop, 1969

Distinguished Woman Award, Delta Theta Sigma Sorority, 1973

Left Bank Jazz Society No. 954 Award, 1974

National Citation, Phi Delta Kappa, Inc. (New Orleans), 1976

Included in Dr. Frances Beckles's *20 Black Women*, 1978

Baltimore's Official Griot, 1983

Keeper of the Flame Award, Maryland Writers' Council, 1983

Twenty Women of Distinction, African-American Women's Political Caucus, 1983

Beautiful Black Woman Award, Towson State University, 1985

Zora Neale Hurston Folklore Award, Association of Black Storytellers, 1985

Installed in Baltimore Great Blacks in Wax Museum, 1989

Included in Ralph Reckley, Sr.'s *20th Century Black American Women in Print*, 1991

Maryland's Official Griot, 1991

America's Mother Griot, National Association of Black Storytellers, 1994

Limited Edition of Mary Carter Smith Mother Griot Doll, 1994

INDEX